MW01206151

***GREAT.
ARE ALSO AVAILABLE IN EBOOR
AND AUDIOBOOK FORMAT.**

GREATER THAN A TOURIST
BOOK SERIES
REVIEWS FROM READERS

I think the series is wonderful and beneficial for tourists to get information before visiting the city.

-Seckin Zumbul, Izmir Turkey

I am a world traveler who has read many trip guides but this one really made a difference for me. I would call it a heartfelt creation of a local guide expert instead of just a guide.

-Susy, Isla Holbox, Mexico

New to the area like me, this is a must have!

-Joe, Bloomington, USA

This is a good series that gets down to it when looking for things to do at your destination without having to read a novel for just a few ideas.

-Rachel, Monterey, USA

Good information to have to plan my trip to this destination.

GREATER THAN A TOURIST- LEWIS-CLARK

VALLEY IDAHO & WASHINGTON

USA

50 Travel Tips from a Local

Steven Hajost

The statements in this book are of the authors and may not be the views of
CZYK Publishing or Greater Than a Tourist.
First Edition
Edited by Eric Whitman
Cover designed by Ivana Stamenkovic
Cover Image: By Dsdugan - Own work, Public Domain,
https://commons.wikimedia.org/w/index.php?curid=3392388

CZYK Publishing Since 2011.
CZYKPublishing.com
Greater Than a Tourist

Lock Haven, PA
All rights reserved.
ISBN: 9798702954936

>TOURIST

50 TRAVEL TIPS FROM A LOCAL

BOOK DESCRIPTION

With travel tips and culture in our guidebooks written by a local, it is never too late to visit The Lewis-Clark Valley. *Greater Than a Tourist- Lewis-Clark Valley USA*, by author Steven Hajost, offers the inside scoop on the beautiful Lewis-Clark Valley. Most travel books tell you how to travel like a tourist. Although there is nothing wrong with that, as part of the *Greater Than a Tourist* series, this book will give you candid travel tips from someone who has lived at your next travel destination. This guide book will not tell you exact addresses or store hours, but instead gives you knowledge that you may not find in other smaller print travel books. Experience cultural, culinary delights and attractions with the guidance of a local. Slow down and get to know the people with this invaluable guide. By the time you finish this book, you will be eager and prepared to discover new activities at your next travel destination.

Inside this travel guide book you will find:

- Visitor information from a local
- Tour ideas and inspiration
- Save time with valuable guidebook information

'Greater Than a Tourist- A Travel Guidebook with 50 Travel Tips from a Local'. Slow down, stay in one place and get to know the people and culture. By the time you finish this book, you will be eager and prepared to travel to your next destination.

OUR STORY

Traveling is a passion of the *Greater Than a Tourist* book series creator. Lisa studied abroad in college, and for their honeymoon Lisa and her husband toured Europe. During her travels to Malta, an older man tried to give her some advice based on his own experience living on the island since he was a young boy. She was not sure if she should talk to the stranger but was interested in his advice. When traveling to some places she was wary to talk to locals because she was afraid that they weren't being genuine. Through her travels, Lisa learned how much locals had to share with tourists. Lisa created the *Greater Than a Tourist* book series to help connect people with locals. A topic that locals are very passionate about sharing.

TABLE OF CONTENTS

16. Hells Gate State Park
17. Chief Timothy Park
18. Fields Spring State Park
19. Smaller Parks
20. Golf
21. Asotin County Aquatic Center
22. GroundWork Brewing
23. Love Shack Kitchen
24. Riverport Brewing Co
25. Lindsay Creek Vineyards
26. Rivaura Estate Vineyard and Winery
27. Twisted Vine Wine Tours
28. Vista House
29. Mystic Cafe
30. Season's Bites and Burgers
31. Brava's
32. Waffles n' More
33. Effies
34. Rooster's Waterfront Restaurant
35. Hanger Mall
36. Newberry Square
37. Skalicky's Sweet Sensations
38. Idaho Memories Gift and Souvenir Shop.
39. Nez Perce Traditions Gift Shop.
40. Hampton Inn
41. Hells Canyon Grand Hotel

DEDICATION

This book is dedicated to my son, Jack. May this one day inspire you to follow your dreams.

ABOUT THE AUTHOR

Steve Hajost lives in Lewiston, Idaho with his wife, son, and dog, Karma. Steve has had the pleasure to call Lewiston, Idaho his home for almost 20 years. Before moving to Lewiston, Idaho in 2003, Steve lived in Davenport, Iowa and before that the Chicago area. Steve enjoys hiking and he has hiked a lot of the trails in the Lewis-Clark Valley area. It is not uncommon for Steve and his family to take a random adventure daytrip. The family normally pick a direction and just go. Steve would like to continue his writing and probably one day break into fiction writing.

HOW TO USE THIS BOOK

The *Greater Than a Tourist* book series was written by someone who has lived in an area for over three months. The goal of this book is to help travelers either dream or experience different locations by providing opinions from a local. The author has made suggestions based on their own experiences. Please check before traveling to the area in case the suggested places are unavailable.

Travel Advisories: As a first step in planning any trip abroad, check the Travel Advisories for your intended destination.
https://travel.state.gov/content/travel/en/traveladvisories/traveladvisories.html

FROM THE PUBLISHER

Traveling can be one of the most important parts of a person's life. The anticipation and memories that you have are some of the best. As a publisher of the *Greater Than a Tourist*, as well as the popular *50 Things to Know* book series, we strive to help you learn about new places, spark your imagination, and inspire you. Wherever you are and whatever you do, I wish you safe, fun and inspiring travel.

Lisa Rusczyk Ed. D.
CZYK Publishing

WELCOME TO
> TOURIST

"Everywhere is within walking distance, if you have the time."

– Steven Wright

When I moved to the Lewis-Clark Valley in 2003, I thought it was just another small town with nothing to offer. I was 19 and had lived in large cities my whole life until that point. Over the past years, I have come to love everything about this valley. The community, history and adventure know no boundary. Every time I think I have found all this area has to offer, another layer is peeled back, and I have a new quest before me. The history of the Lewis-Clark Valley dates back to times before it was called the Lewis-Clark Valley. The Nimiipuu Indians have called this land their home for 11,000 years. Pick a direction and drive 30 mins and find your new favorite adventure spot. If you do not want to leave town, explore the miles of walking and hiking trails in town. Sit on the deck at one of our local restaurants, brewhouses or wineries for some good music and great views. I have yet to find another place like this and I'm not sure I ever want to look.

As I said before, this land has layers upon layers of rich history. There are underground tunnels, secret rooms, hidden gems. Every place explored turns up more questions and every question will lead to a grand adventure. While Lewiston, Idaho was at one point the Idaho capital, it was not the first capital of the territory. Lewis and Clark slept on the banks of both Lewiston and Clarkston while exploring the new territory. Spaulding, Idaho had a hand in developing Mickey Mouse and shaping the Disney Universe into what we know it as today. Before any of that history, the Nimiipuu tribe roamed these lands. There are hundreds of historical markers all over these lands. Soaking in all the history is worth any adventure that awaits those willing to wander.

One must come prepared for an adventure if they are going to see everything the Lewis-Clark Valley area offers. Every answer leads to a new trail, cave, or abandoned town to explore. My adventure in the Lewis-Clark Valley started with a simple walk along the river. I met a new friend and was told about a trail that led up to some hot springs. "It's about half a day's hike to get to them, but the soak is worth it", I was told. I got to those hot springs the following weekend and met some people who not only knew their hiking trails, but the history of the trails. I have been hooked ever since. What started as a simple walk turned into me wanting to see and know all the valley has to offer.

The Lewis-Clark Valley area is proof the world was at one point much smaller than we realize. I moved here not knowing anyone. I met some friends, started hanging out with them, then it turned out or grandfathers did not serve directly with each other in WWII, but were there at the same time. Then upon researching, find out I have an 8th cousin that lived in this very area when it was still a territory. Most places have a seven-degrees of separation game, the Lewis-Clark Valley has a three-degrees of separation rule. Nobody in this valley is disconnected by more than three people.

Will I ever see everything the Lewis-Clark Valley has to offer? Probably not. However, I can't wait for my next adventure or friend I make or fact I learn. I'm excited for my son to grow up here and discover the things I've learned. I hope you are ready, too. Please, visit my home, make some new friends and learn all you can on your adventure. Get hooked on this valley the way I did in 2003, when I thought I would never stay here. This land is full of wilderness to be explored or to simply get lost in. I know it's a bit cliché, but this is where you come to get your head right.

1. CONFLUENCE CENTER

Located along the Lewiston Levee, near the confluence of the Snake and Clearwater Rivers. The center marks the campsite of the Lewis and Clark Expedition on October 10, 1805. The center offers a small pavilion that hosts a timeline of the Lewis-Clark Expedition. There are several pieces of art, including a hand-cut canoe and a bronze fountain dedicated to Sacajawea. The area behind the Confluence Center also offers some of the best fishing spots one could ask for. A friend and I used to walk the Lewiston Levee Trail every night after work. Our first resting point was always the Confluence Center. Listening to the trickle of the fountain or sitting on the dock and staring out into the convergence of two rivers is oddly satisfying. There is a parking lot at the end of D Street and a pedestrian bridge for those who don't want to walk too far.

2. HELLS CANYON RESORT AND MARINA

The Lewis-Clark Valley offers several miles of walking trails, including the Lewiston and Clarkston Levees. If one were to leave the Confluence Center and walk across the Blue Bridge and follow the Clarkston Levee west, they would find themselves at the Marina, located at 1560 Port Drive in Clarkston. While the stunning river views on the walk to the Marina are worth the effort, Hells Canyon Resort and Marina host some awesome sidewalk etchings depicting the Lewis and Clark Expedition. The etchings will satisfy both art and history buffs alike. Later in this book, I will mention several more places to stop along this same path. For now, let's talk about the Marina itself. It is rated in the top 100 RV parks in America. They have an indoor pool and hot tub, onsite laundry facilities, and full RV hook-ups. The Marina is a great place to dock a boat or park an RV for a bit of around-town fun. Keep in mind that the Lewis-Clark Valley is the furthest inland seaport in the United States, making the Lewis-Clark Valley even accessible by boat.

3. NEZ PERCE COUNTY HISTORICAL MUSEUM

Located at 306 Third Street, The museum acts as a satellite location for the Lewis-Clark Valley Visitor Center. The museum is dedicated to the collection, preservation and dissemination of area history and historical artifacts. The Nez Perce County Historical Museum hosts a plethora of artifacts, stories and pictures of the valley from its founding as a territory to modern times. One of the exhibits I feel is a must-see is The Trolley Car #8, which is one of the three original trolley cars used in the valley. The exhibit tells people the route the car took, it's years of use, how it was used and why it was phased out. There are also passages on the manufacturer of the car, including peak production years. The Nez Perce County Historical Society has done all they can to share the history of the Lewis-Clark Valley area. One can even visit their website for a brief history of the local area. This museum was one of the first stops I made when I moved to the valley, the first layer so to speak. I encourage all who visit the Lewis-Clark Valley to check out the museum before they start their adventure.

4. IDAHO HISTORY TOURS

The history of Lewiston's underground is a fascinating one, to say the least. Lewiston was born out of the "wild west", which means there was a bit of lawlessness in the beginning. There are secret brothels and gambling dens all over downtown, some of which were attached to normal businesses. Idaho History Tours feature a walking tour of downtown Lewiston. Garry Bush will tell the tales of over 100 years of Lewiston History. The tour will include the tunnels that exist below the city of Lewiston. The tunnels are said to be haunted by the "unmentionables" in society at the time. Garry will also provide documented haunted activity for each building entered. I have not gotten a chance to take the tour yet, it's a regret. I tell myself every year I'm going to find some people who want to go with me, but somehow always find an excuse. I can assure you I will be taking this tour soon. I'm sure my curiosity will be triggered and I will need to dive deeper into the Lewis-Clark Valley history. If the tour sounds exciting, remember to reserve a spot on their website before you get here. The tour company even offers a special Halloween tour focusing on the haunted side of downtown Lewiston. Though the guide cannot promise you'll see a ghost, they also make you sign a waiver in case you do.

.

5. JACK O'CONNOR HUNTING HERITAGE AND EDUCATION CENTER

Jack O'Connor was a well-known author, outdoorsman and shooter. He was best known for his work in *Outdoor Life* magazine, he also wrote several non-fiction books. According to Jack's son, Bradford, Jack wrote more than 1200 articles for various magazines, including *Esquire* and *Cosmopolitan*. He was an English professor in Texas before leaving to write full-time in 1945. Jack moved to Lewiston, Idaho in 1948, where he lived until he died in 1978. In 2006, Hells Gate State Park opened The Jack O'Connor Hunting and Heritage Education Center. The mission of the center is to provide, promote and foster educational opportunities inspired by Jack O'Connor's vision as a noted outdoorsman, author, hunter and conservationist. Many of Jack O'Connor's videos and literature on the region are available at the center. They also offer scavenger hunts for all ages. The Center is a fun place to visit for all ages. The center is also accessible from the southern part of the Lewiston Levee pathway.

6. VALLEY ART CENTER

Located in Clarkston, The Valley Art Center focuses on supporting and encouraging arts in the Lewis-Clark Valley. They do this by displaying the works of local artists and offering to sell their works. The Center also offers various classes and workspaces for the artists to create their masterpieces. The Center is open to the public and offers a wide range of original gifts and pieces. If I'm being honest, I had never entered the Center until a month or two ago, when my wife stopped in to see if she wanted to sell her art in the Center. I'm not now, nor have I ever been a good artist, but I have always appreciated good art. The various styles and media used can be a bit overwhelming, but in a good way. There is something to please any eye in the gallery. If the gallery does not have what you are looking for, check out the back room that is full of workspaces the artists can rent while they do their work. I enjoyed my walk through the center and look forward to future visits.

7. NEZ PERCE NATIONAL HISTORICAL PARK

Located just outside Lewiston is the Nez Perce National Park. The park is a quiet and peaceful little spot where one can learn about Nimiipuu's history and culture. The headquarters of the park features clothing, hand dug-out canoes and an ancient lodge. The park acquired its first collection from Watson's Store and Evens Sacajawea Museum in 1965. The park began the formal collections management program in 1977. The program also curates' collections from several other National Park Service sites. The park also offers a virtual museum on its website. My wife and I frequent this park. It is beautiful and tranquil. The old buildings have an eerie calm. I highly recommend checking out the Spaulding's Mission. All that remains is some fenced-off foundation stones. However, the site once featured a home, a school and a printing house all built by Henry and Eliza Spaulding in the summer of 1838. The Spaulding's story is an interesting one, to say the least, and well worth the read. There is a great walking path that runs through the park for those who would like to put in a set of headphones and explore.

8. CLEARWATER RIVER CASINO

Looking for a nice place to stay and relax a bit while touring the Lewis-Clark Valley? Consider the Clearwater River Casino. The hotel side offers 50 non-smoking rooms, a saltwater pool, spa plus a full-service restaurant. The Casino also offers an RV park with 21 full hook-up sites. Their sports bar is a great place to watch any sporting event. They also have an event center with concerts, comedy shows and MMA fights. The 21-and-up casino floor features over 600 games with weekly special events. The Qeqiit Restaurant offers both upscale and casual dishes that can satisfy any need. Not hungry enough for a meal? Hit the Yawwinma Café for a snack. After dinner, hit the casino's cultural walk, which features stories of the 11,000-year Nez Perce history. The casino is a great place to get lost for a day or two.

9. HELLS CANYON

Hells Canyon is North America's deepest river gorge. The canyon was cut by the Snake River and made famous when Evel Knievel attempted to jump the gorge. Though his jump site was further south, Hells Canyon still offers a plethora of activities while staying in the Lewis-Clark Valley. Fishing, kayaking, and jetboat tours are all a possibility in Hells Canyon. There are several ghost towns and original homesteads along the river. You can choose between self-exploratory and guided tours. One of my favorite uses of the canyon is floating. I have discovered so many random caves and pathways by simply kicking back in a raft and letting the world float by. There are several old claims and such along the riverbanks, where gems can still be found. I think the best part of floating is that I'm allowed to explore at my own pace. If you do not have much experience floating, I suggest you take a guide or someone experienced with you. It's really easy to get sucked into an eddy when you don't know what to look out for.

10. JET BOAT TOURS

If you want to take in all the river has to offer in one day, you should choose one of three jet boat tours. The boats will take you several miles up and down Hells Canyon. You'll see caves, abandoned homesteads and ghost towns. You'll learn the history behind all these sites and what makes them so special to the local area. Snake River Adventures provides my favorite tour. They offer a full-day or half-day trips. The guides will give all the information about Hells Canyon - from history to flora to geology - they know it all. Snake River Adventures also offer wine tours and fishing excursions. The tours can be a bit pricey, but well worth the cost. I recommend a Jet Boat tour as a "must-do" activity when visiting the LC Valley.

11. KAYAKING TRIPS

If jet boats are not your thing, consider a guided kayaking trip. Several guides can be hired for a day. Some of the guides have just as much, if not more information about the area. I have yet to try a kayak trip on the Snake River, but it is on my list of things to do. I would love to spend more time exploring caves or abandoned ghost towns. There are also a few restaurants I would like to try that are easily accessible from a dock. Make a point to check out Heller Bar. You will not regret the scenery or the fishing.

12. RIVER RAFTING TRIPS

If venturing to the Lewis-Clark Valley for some adventure, try out a rafting trip. There are a few different companies and clubs that will allow anyone of any experience to run the river with them. They know all the best rafting spots. The Clearwater River offers the most fun rapids in the area. If you show up at the right time, you can help out with the river clean-up each year. The river clean-up is sponsored by local clubs and companies, so there are generally prize giveaways while being of service to the community.

13. FISHING

The Lewis-Clark Valley area offers hundreds of miles of river banks, dozens of lakes, and even a pond or two. We have steelhead, salmon, trout, catfish, sturgeon, and much more depending on where you decide to fish. If you're not sure what you would like to fish for, several guided tours will show the best spots and equipment to use. The record catfish to come out of the Valley is 38 inches long and 31.05 pounds. The record sturgeon was close to 14 feet long and weighed over 400 pounds. This is an angler's paradise. In 2009, Lewiston, Idaho was named Outdoor Life's top town for sportsmen. Lewiston has dropped a few notches over time, but has remained in the top 10 and has also been added to the list of other hunting and fishing magazines.

14. HUNTING

As stated previously, Lewiston, Idaho has been on the top-ten list for most sportsmen magazines for years. At one point they were the number one town for sportsmen. There is something for every hunter in the area. We have bobcats, wolves, bears and elk. The region is home to the largest wilderness lands in the lower 48 states. Much of these lands can only be accessed by foot, boat or horseback. You'll need to be ready if you are going to hunt in this area. If you're unsure of your prowess or just want to get a good feel for the area you can always hire a guide that will pick you up and show you the best way to prepare for the task ahead. The guide will also take you out into the best spot to bag whatever trophy you're looking for. If you are not experienced in the local wilderness, I implore you to take a guide. It is very easy to get lost and/or stuck in this area. I've even seen experienced locals end up lost and confused.

15. BIKING

Mountain, road or casual bike adventures can be found in almost any direction of the valley. The Lewis-Clark Valley offers over 25 miles of paved bike trails, even more unpaved bike adventures. The mountain trails are said to be some of the best, though I have not personally ridden them. Some road bikers like to travel our country roads or one of the scenic highways in the area. Try your hand at the annual "I Made the Grade" bike race - 8 miles of uphill switchbacks. Set into the Lewiston Hill, the top of the hill will offer a breathtaking view of the entire valley and surrounding lands.

16. HELLS GATE STATE PARK

Hells Gate State Park offers a little bit to entertain everyone. They have rentable cabins, campsites and RV hook-ups. The park offers art, museums, beaches, horse trails and disk golf. I have personally walked every inch of every trail in this park and love it. There is always a sight to see. Local wildlife can be found everywhere. The art exhibits are fantastic and sometimes the employees put on campfire stories. Even though I have hiked every trail, the terrain is always changing, helping me to find something new to explore. Sitting on a bench at the top of The Devils Slide allows one to see straight down the mouth of Hells Canyon. The park staff offer many activities to please their guests. My favorite thing about the park is that it starts the Lewiston side of the Levee Trail. As I stated before, a person could spend days exploring the levee trails. There are so many sites and places along the trail, it's hard to narrow the Lewis-Clark Valley down to 50 things. Maybe I'll write another book with 50 things to see and do on the Lewis-Clark Levee Trails. Getting back to Hells Gate State Park itself, the various history and art centers are worth taking a day to explore the sites.

17. CHIEF TIMOTHY PARK

Located about 8 miles west of Clarkston is Chief Timothy Park. The park features kayak rentals, beaches and playgrounds. Chief Timothy features my favorite beach. The sand is warm, the water cool and the sun can always be seen. My son played in the river for the first time at this park. I have yet to rent one of their kayaks, but I have friends who have and enjoy their time. I plan to try this adventure this summer - at the very least I will have a story. The amount of beach the park offers is dependent on how high the river is running.

18. FIELDS SPRING STATE PARK

Prepare to be amazed by Fields Spring State Park. Stay in the lodge or in one of the 8-person tepees while you explore the 826-acre forested mountain park. I have never been to this park. I didn't even know of this park until this past fall. I now plan to go check it out when the weather agrees. I've been told the park offers some of the best views of the Blues Mountain Range one could ever ask for. A coworker informed me that Fields Spring State Park offers some of the best hiking trails for avid-fans or beginners. I assure any readers I will be going to Fields Spring State Park this summer and pictures will be posted on my Facebook page. I may even shoot some video.

19. SMALLER PARKS

The Lewis-Clark Valley also offers several smaller parks in town. Each park has its own personality and history in the valley. I try and take my son to a different park each weekend. My favorite park to take him to is Sunset Park. I like Sunset Park because it has a variety of activities such as swings, baseball fields, soccer fields and musical instruments to play with. The slides are his favorite thing to play on. If you visit around the holiday season, you'll see Locomotive Park lit up with the most impressive display of lights in town.

20. GOLF

Lewiston and Clarkston both offer several golf courses, each with a unique setting and style. I am not an avid golfer. However, my in-laws are, and they tend to like Bryden Canyon the best for in-town golfing. I know the food at the Lewiston Country Club is fantastic. Most of the clubs in the valley offer cart rental and caddy services.

21. ASOTIN COUNTY AQUATIC CENTER

Show up in the warmer weather and you'll find the Asotin County Family Aquatic Center fully open. The park offers waterslides, a lazy river and a wave pool. They also offer a full gym with day passes inside, along with a pool and hot tub. I like taking my son to the Center when it's warmer. The children's pool has several sprinkler and waterfall features that he enjoys.

22. GROUNDWORK BREWING

Groundwork is the newest local brewery, and they are making some amazing concoctions. Check them out for good beer and live music. Sit and watch the crowd gather from the houses above the brewery. Groundwork brings in a different band each weekend while slinging their brews. The prices are fairly inexpensive, too. Their mead is great on a warm summer night. They generally offer amazing flatbread pizzas. However, if that is not your taste, a local food truck is parked about 50 feet away and ready to serve the best St Louis-style BBQ this side of the mountains. I can't say enough about how great this place is or the people who own it. It is worth every penny spent in their establishment.

23. LOVE SHACK KITCHEN

Now that I talked about Groundwork Brewing, I have to talk about the food truck that partnered with the brewery. Love Shack Kitchen makes some of the most delicious BBQ in town. The staff is friendly and all the sides are made in house. Their Mac-N-Cheese is out of this world, as are their ribs. They make four different sauces to put on their various BBQ products. You will not leave this place hungry, as the portions are way bigger than the prices. Grab some pulled pork and walk over to the deck at Groundwork for a fun, relaxing and full night.

24. RIVERPORT BREWING CO

Riverport was one of the first breweries in the Lewis-Clark Valley. There, River Rat Red can be found in the many restaurants and bars throughout the valley. Riverport is always putting on some kind of special event. It could be a comic book and record swap; they might be running a charity night. Generally, they just put on some great music to go along with their local brews. The best part about Riverport is that it's not too far from that walking path we talked about earlier in the book. It's situated halfway between the Blue Bridge and the Marina, so stop in and take a rest in between your sight-seeing adventures.

25. LINDSAY CREEK VINEYARDS

Lindsay Creek is one of the many local vineyards. They host events and have a breath-taking view of the Lewis-Clark Valley countryside. My wife and I generally head over that way for one of the many charity events they host. Their finger foods partner well with their wines. If you find you like Lindsay Creek's products, you can join their wine club. The staff is friendly and always have a suggestion for the patrons that are unsure of what they want. I like to order a random flight, just for a surprise. I've never fully liked wine until I learned about it from Lindsay Creek. You can generally find their specials and a list of events on their website or on their Facebook page.

26. RIVAURA ESTATE VINEYARD AND WINERY

It's often said that great people make great wine, and that is the case with Rivaura. The Hewett family are top-notch and do make wine that is loved all over this valley. Found on both banks of the Clearwater River, Rivaura offers several blends of wine. They have a wine club with special members-only events. Their tasting room is about 30 mins. south-east in Julietta, Idaho and is open Wednesday through Sunday. While I'm not a wine guru, my wife kind of is and she loves Rivaura wines.

27. TWISTED VINE WINE TOURS

Not sure which winery you want to visit in the Lewis-Clark Valley? Try them all. Twisted Vine will take a group of 2 to 7 people on a tour of the local wineries while teaching the wine history of the valley. Twisted Vine Tours was started several years ago by Clint Hoiland. Clint never liked wine until he tasted a few good wines and learned more about the subject. He was hooked. He started learning all that he could. One day, after a suggestion from a friend, he started a wine tour company to pass on his knowledge. Clint not only likes the wine but the stories behind the wine. He would like to share those stories with visitors of the Lewis-Clark Valley. Tours range in price, depending on how much time and how many vineyards are visited.

28. VISTA HOUSE

The Vista House was at one point a gift and souvenir shop. The current owners purchased it in 2016 and hoped to turn it into a convenience store and event space with a wine and beer bar/ tasting room. They remodeled the place and turned it into an event center with the most stunning view of the entire valley. The owners/hosts are kind, amazing people who ensure all their guests have the best time possible. The Vista House has long been a historic facility in the Lewis-Clark Valley. Thanks to the new owners, it will continue to bring joy for the future generations to come. My wife and I were at the Vista House this past summer for a small wedding venue. It was the first time I had set foot in the Vista House for quite some time. It looked wonderful. No expense was held back in its update. You'll have a sense of awe, staring out into the furthest reaches of the Lewis-Clark Valley.

29. MYSTIC CAFE

Mystic Café is a fabulous little spot for a lunch date. They feature a plethora of beers and wines. In the evenings, they feature live music and local poets. Lunch menus generally feature simple soups, sandwiches and salads. At night, they break out the steaks and the pasta. Their mustard rotini is one of my favorite dishes on the menu, however, the mushrooms will always be number one in my book. Mystic also serves as a small fresh coffee shop during the day. Their coffee is always fresh and delicious

30. SEASON'S BITES AND BURGERS

Season's Bites and Burgers is located in one of the most historic downtown buildings. Their bite-size steak is always mouthwatering and on-point. The restaurant also offers hand-patted burgers with fresh, local ingredients. They always have local beer and wine, along with weekend specials. My wife and I are semi-foodies (well, we love good food, to say the least). I was thrilled when I found out Season's offered small cooking classes. I plan to treat my wife to some of these classes for our anniversary. I also plan to take their sushi class for myself.

31. BRAVA'S

One simply cannot come to the Lewis-Clark Valley and not try Brava's. They got new owners a few years ago and it was just what the place needed. The new owners kept most of the menu but started offering fresh daily lunch and dinner specials. The full-service bar in the back offers plenty of great cocktails that pair with any meal. My wife likes to play their wine roulette - you simply tell them red or white and they pick the wine for you. I recently decided to try all the various original specialty cocktails they offer. I have never had a bad meal in this establishment. They knock it out of the park every time. The staff is always friendly and willing to help a new customer find their new favorite dish. Their chocolate cake is rich and divine. You can't lose in this place, no matter what you order.

32. WAFFLES N' MORE

Waffles n' More is a staple in the Lewis-Clark Valley. They are a classic American-style diner that has been serving this valley since long before I came here. Their waitstaff is top-notch when it comes to customer service. The menu features something that can please everyone. Come hungry because the portions are huge. While I have been slowly working my way down the list of all their various waffles, the country fried steak skillet remains my favorite thing on the menu. Expect a wait if you show up on a weekend or while any events are happening in the valley. The only way to leave this place hungry is to actively try.

33. EFFIES

Are you a burger fan? How about redundantly huge burgers? If you answered yes to either question then it's time you try and conquer an Effie. One of their burgers features 4 pounds of meat. Most of their sides are house-made and the people are great. The diner is said to have been a favorite of actor Charles

Bronson. The sign for the place also made it into the movie "The River Thief." In 2020, the original owners sold Effies to the current owners. The new owners kept the business model as is - fresh beef never frozen and eight-inch buns. The new owners added a few differently topped burgers plus some other small things. You can feed a small army for not that much money. I challenge you to put down an entire Effie. You can work off the food by walking the Levee Path after.

34. ROOSTER'S WATERFRONT RESTAURANT

Roosters sit along the river path on the Clarkston side of the river. It's roughly three-quarters of the way between the Blue Bridge and the Marina. I recommend it as a great place to stop and rest between the two sites. Roosters has a great deck with magnificent river views and live music on the weekend evenings. Roosters offers 18 rotating Micro Brews, 15 different wines, and some well-crafted drinks. My wife prefers the mojitos. The appetizers at Roosters are well crafted and satisfy any taste.

Everyone is bound to find something they like at Roosters. Their broad menu offers anything from steaks to pasta. I highly recommend Roosters Blueberry BBQ Ribs. The ribs are fall off the bone tender and the sauce is simply perfect in taste. Roosters is a great place to take a quick break with a beer or glass of wine. It is also a fun place to grab dinner and enjoy some live music.

35. HANGER MALL

What started life in 1938 as a small airport, was later shut down and reimagined as something entirely different. As stated before, The Asotin County Airport started life in 1938 and was not fully recognized until 1945, when it was finally put onto a few maps. The runway was said to be about 3400 feet and spanned east to west. The airport has been altered throughout the years, eventually becoming the Hanger Mall. The mall is not too far off the Levee Path and is a hop, skip and a jump away from Roosters. You'll find antiques, gifts and local crafts galore in this wonderful building. I like to meander the aisles for the nostalgia (I've always been able to find something that takes me back to my childhood).

There are also pictures of the airfield in its heyday along the walls. The Hanger Mall is a nice stop for someone looking to get lost for a bit and take in the history of the Lewis-Clark Valley.

36. NEWBERRY SQUARE

Newberry Square is a hidden gem located in downtown Lewiston. The building started life as J.J. Newberry Co. and it operated until its closure in 1977. The building was later purchased and restored by Nikky and Vikky Ross. The Ross sisters added several different shops to the restored building. The Square features a restaurant, bakery, gift shops, winery and a tea shop. There is a little something for everyone to enjoy in Newberry Square. Stop in for a quick lunch and leave with an Idaho t-shirt. The bakery is so good, but we will get into that next.

37. SKALICKY'S SWEET SENSATIONS

One of the offerings of Newberry Square is Skalicky's Sweet Sensations Bakery. Their baked goods are heavenly. The tea and coffee products are okay. They also take special orders. It's hard to decide if I like the turnovers or the tarts the best. All I know is that I have always left Skalicky's fatter and happier. My son had his first cinnamon roll here at their open-house. They offer keto and gluten-free items if that's what you are looking for. Don't skip the lemon cupcakes. You'll regret it later.

38. IDAHO MEMORIES GIFT AND SOUVENIR SHOP

After tasting the treats from Skalicky's, stop into Idaho Memories Gift and Souvenir Shop. The shop offers everything Idaho is known for or anything they can find made in Idaho. The staff always makes the customers feel welcome. One will find a wide variety of items in this shop, from huckleberry items to gemstones. I enjoy making some of the various prepackaged recipe mixes I find in the shop; I have vowed to try them all. The lentil cookies are out-of-this-world good to make at home. You can also find all your Idaho needs in this shop. Most all of the local history books can be found in the shop, too. I recommend anything by Steve Branting.

39. NEZ PERCE TRADITIONS GIFT SHOP.

Across the hall from Idaho Memories is the Nez Perce Traditions Gift Shop. This shop specializes in hand-made goods. The staff is friendly and knowledgeable. One can find anything from hand-made soap and baskets to clothing and jewelry. The shop staff can also help you connect with tours that specifically follow the history and culture of the Nimiipuu. Stop in and find the many beautiful items the shop has to offer and ask them about the history of their people and how they helped forge the Lewis-Clark Valley into what it is today.

40. HAMPTON INN

Hampton Inn is among the newest hotels in the Lewis-Clark Valley. Each room is beautiful with some comfortable rooms. They offer free wi-fi, breakfast and shuttle from the airport. The hotel also features a fitness center, meeting rooms and an indoor heated pool. You can relax on their deck that overlooks the Snake and Clearwater River Canyons. The lobby is bright and inviting with plenty of free coffee. I have had family that have stayed at this hotel a few times. I can assure you the beds are relaxing and the hotel staff goes above and beyond the call of duty to ensure every guest feels like they have a second home at The Hampton Inn.

41. HELLS CANYON GRAND HOTEL

The Hells Canyon Grand Hotel is one of the biggest hotels most see when entering Lewiston, Idaho. The rooms are modern and sleek, featuring wi-fi, work desks, coffee makers, plush beds and complimentary hot breakfasts. The hotel lobby also features two bars, a restaurant, and a big deck with live events every weekend. The hotel staff will hook you up with just about everything you need and could want to do for entertainment. There is a full indoor and outdoor event center with several smaller meeting rooms. In the Christmas season, guests will be treated to a fantastic view of the locomotive park lights. Snap Fitness is located just across the parking lot and partners with the hotel guests. Meriweather's Bistro is located on the ground floor of the hotel and will cook up some great food. The house chips have to be my favorite item on the menu, although, everything on the menu exceeds expectations. MJ Barley Hoppers can help any guest wet their whistle. The deck is open throughout the summer and features live music most every weekend. The hotel was recently purchased in 2021 and is in the process of being upgraded throughout, meaning there will be more great things to come from this hotel. I highly suggest anyone to stay here. The food is great, the staff is friendly, and the atmosphere is relaxing.

42. HOLIDAY INN

Holiday Inn recently purchased a hotel located on the river path in Clarkston, Washington. I highly enjoyed the hotel it was before Holiday Inn. Their food was great, the staff was always friendly, there is a driving range and a mini-golf course behind the hotel, and every summer there is a concert for charity. I have not stayed in the hotel since it was bought, but I can only imagine that Holiday Inn enhanced these things. The IGH group spent most of 2020 renovating the hotel inside and out. The 24-hour fitness center will get anyone ready to tackle the day. They also feature a full business center, live entertainment, cocktail lounge, laundry site, wi-fi and safety deposit boxes. Their restaurant is top-notch, including the desserts. The staff is quick to help with any problem and the river views are stunning. The Holiday Inn is located on the River Levee Path I have talked about in this book before. I suggest the Holiday Inn to anyone wanting to enjoy a day trip walking the path.

43. BEST WESTERN PLUS: THE INN AT HELLS CANYON

Built-in 2020, the Best Western Plus: The Inn at Hells Canyon is the newest hotel in the Lewis-Clark Valley. I have only been to this hotel for their grand opening and I can say it left me in awe. The lobby is bright and features a creative tribute to the area. The breakfast and snack areas are beautiful and feature great pieces of art. The rooms are simple, elegant and welcoming. They also have an indoor heated pool, fitness room, breakfast, business center, laundry facility and kitchenette suites. The Inn at Hells Canyon has gone above and beyond to show its guests what the spirit of the Lewis-Clark Valley is all about. I'm sure it will become a favorite place for you to stay as well.

44. HOT AUGUST NIGHTS

Hot August Nights is an event that has been held in the Valley since 1987. What started as an event to bring music to the valley eventually turned into a classic car show with concerts and shows galore. Hot August Nights are truly the Lewis-Clark community at its finest. A local car dealership kicks off the week-long event with a show-n-shine. The following weekend, downtown streets are closed off for the classic car show and nightly cruise. The event is finished with a concert at Boomers Garden. The whole community comes together for the event and makes it a true sight to see in Lewiston, Idaho. Hot August Nights takes place the last weekend of August each year in the Lewis-Clark Valley and is a true sight to see. In recent years, the nightly cruise has moved on from just classic cars, adding in custom cars. My favorite car to date is the modified Flintstones car a local person made and enters every year. Being a part of the Inland Pacific area means there is no shortage of custom street rods.

45. THE NAIA WORLD SERIES OF BASEBALL.

Held every year since 1957, the NAIA World Series is a fun event that has been hosted by Lewis-Clark State College for the past 20 of those 64 years. The tournament is a double-elimination event to determine the National Association of Intercollegiate Athletics (NAIA) champion. Twelve cities have hosted the tournament, none as long as the Lewis-Clark Valley. Every hotel, restaurant and shop are full for the week of the World Series. The whole town gets involved with special events, live music and sidewalk events downtown. Every coach, player and parent who visits the Valley during this event is made to feel welcomed and comfortable. Many have been here for several years and call it their "summer home." The Lewis-Clark Valley is at its best for that week and is truly remarkable. The tournament kicks off every Memorial Day weekend and ends the following weekend. If you are into baseball or enjoy a bustling smaller town atmosphere, Memorial Day weekend is the time you want to visit the Lewis-Clark Valley.

46. THE DOGWOOD FESTIVAL

The Dogwood Festival is a community event that has been held in the Lewis-Clark Valley since 1985. The celebration includes an art show featuring all media types, an elementary art show, beer and wine tasting, an artisan fair with hundreds of booths and the Seaport River Run. The festival takes place in several locations all over town, depending on the event and the sponsor. I look forward to my son getting old enough for the dog show hosted by Lewis-Clark Kennel Club. Jack loves dogs and would be excited to see them in all shapes and sizes. My wife loves the Art Under the Elms event or the craft fair. Hundreds of booths filled with hand-crafted soaps, spices, art and jewelry. There is normally an entire block of food trucks from all over the region. The whole week turns out to be a fun discovery. There is a little something for everyone at the Dogwood Festival. You'll have to keep watch on their website for the dates.

47. GEM HUNTING

There are plenty of ways to make a living in the Lewis-Clark Valley. One of the oldest that still exists today is mining. While the operations are not nearly as big as they once were, I know many people who go explore old claim sites and bring home buckets of garnets, emeralds, even a ruby or two. I have two raw garnets I keep in a collection that I found while out exploring. I started exploring by asking some of the people at the local gem shows where the best places to gem hunt in the valley were. From the advice I got, I discovered the Emerald Creek Garnet area in the Idaho Panhandle National Forest. Though garnets are already rare, Idaho is one of two places in the world one can find star garnets. The garnets must feature the right trace minerals and be cut in a very specific way to produce a 3D-like effect in the garnet itself. I plan on taking a hike this summer to an old abandoned gold claim a friend told me about. Even if I don't find any gold in the area, the hike should be worth it. If you do not want to hike and search, stop by St. Maries, Idaho to view these amazing works of nature.

48. COLLEGES

There are about 7 colleges within 100 miles of the Lewis-Clark Valley: WSU, U of I, LCSC, WWCC, Gonzaga, EWU, and SCC. With all the colleges within a couple of hours drive, there is always some form of entertainment. Concerts, comedy shows, plays and many other events can be found in the region. It's been a few years, but my favorite event I ever attended was on the campus of Washington State University. Frank Warren brought his PostSecret talk to the town. He told his story and what brought him to WSU that day. He then let many people stand up at a microphone and unload the secrets that have been plaguing their lives up to that point. The event combined art and psychology into something much greater. I'll never forget that night, nor the people who shared what drew them to the mic that night. Being so close to these college campuses opens a whole new world of entertainment and memories.

49. THE ROUND-UP

I told you before that every Memorial Day weekend, the Lewis-Clark Valley hosts the NAIA World Series to kick-off the summer season. To close it every Labor Day weekend, Lewiston hosts the Round-Up. A week-long rodeo event that once again brings the community together to celebrate. Cowboys and cowgirls compete to see who the best in the region is. Each night hosts different rodeo events. Saturday kicks off with an early morning downtown parade. The shops, restaurants and streets are once again full of people coming out to root on their favorite PBR hopeful. The atmosphere is a bit different for the week of the Round-Up, but it's still fun and entertaining. The locals trade dusty old ball caps and Carhartt's for Stetsons and Levi's. The entire town becomes a sea of cow-folk as far as the eye can see. Every evening they pile into the rodeo grounds, just outside of town, to see who will conquer the arena. The energy in the area is off the charts and everyone has a good time. It's one of the best events to visit the valley for.

50. LILLIAN DISNEY

Lillian Bounds was born in 1899 in Spaulding, Idaho. By 1925, she would come to be known as Lillian Disney, after working for Disney Studios in "ink and paint" for a brief time. Walt and Lillian were married in 1925 here in Lewiston, Idaho. Lillian is credited with naming Disney's most famous character, Mickey Mouse. Though Walt did not visit much, Lillian is said to have made regular trips to the Lewis-Clark Valley. Though never confirmed, it's rumored that the valley featured at the start of each Disney movie is a model of the Lewis-Clark Valley. Interesting follow-up: Upon further research, it turns out I am related to Lillian by 23 family separations. Thus, proving it's a small world after all. (ha-ha, I had to)

TOP REASONS TO BOOK THIS TRIP

History: The Lewis-Clark Valley is rich in history. A history that dates back long before Lewis and Clark roamed these lands. The area as a whole does its part to preserve as much of the rich history as can be done. There are original mining and logging ghost towns that still stand today because the outside community volunteers their time and effort to ensure future generations can see them too. Up toward Elk River is an entire wagon train road that has been preserved and cared for since the days of the Pony Express. The United States of America may be a young country to the rest of the world, but the Nimiipuu heritage in this valley dates back thousands of years. I learn something new each time I venture out for a random day trip and I am always hungry for more.

Community: The community spirit of the valley is an awesome sight to behold. Every festival, event or fundraiser brings everyone out in droves. We tend to treat all travelers and explorers as our neighbors. We tell them the best restaurant for their craving, the best fishing spot for whatever they want to catch and the best trail to hike for their experience. The people of the Lewis-Clark Valley are not generally greedy in any way. We want everyone to have the best time possible while visiting our home. There are some places you can live and never meet someone in your lifetime. Then there is the LC Valley, where you are bound to run into someone you know whatever you do. It may have been a year since you have seen the person, but it will be like you just talked to them yesterday. I moved to Lewiston, Idaho in 2003, and met some people I now get the privilege of calling family, blood or otherwise because that is how great this community is. Once you look a person in the eye and say hello, you'll have a friend for life.

Exploration: I've lived in the Lewis-Clark Valley for almost 20 years. I moved here from Davenport, Iowa and Chicago, Illinois before that. Never in my life have I explored a place and come out with more questions that lead to more exploration. I always find a new path to explore that leads to a new cave, lake or trail. Every path has a long-standing history in this area. Maybe it was used by settlers to get their horses a drink; maybe it was a trade route 100 years ago and has since been abandoned. I found the way to start peeling the layers back is to ask the experts in this area - 60-and-70-year-old men who have lifetimes of knowledge of the Lewis-Clark Valley region. They have walked almost every path, looked in every cave they could find, and got told every story from their fathers and grandfathers. There are areas of wilderness here only accessible by foot and areas where you can see every star in the sky. There are sights to behold that a cellphone camera could never show and memories to be made that can never be forgotten. This is one of the last few places left in this world a person can get truly lost if they wanted to.

DID YOU KNOW?

-Lewiston Idaho is the furthest inland seaport at 465
        miles in from the sea.

-Though the Disneys never lived in Lewiston
        together, Lillian made regular trips to the
        valley up until her death.

- Lewiston was the Capital of the Idaho Territory
        from 1863 until 1865, when Boise was named
        the capital.

- Lewiston, Idaho is Idaho's lowest point, at about
        738 feet above sea level.

- Lewiston Hill is the highest point at 2,756 feet of
        elevation.

- Lewiston's Old Spiral Highway was built in 1917
        and was used exclusively until the new
        highway was built in 1977.

- Old Spiral Highway is still the hill of choice for
        anyone wanting to take their time or on a
        motorcycle.

- The Lewis-Clark Valley features a "mild but wild"
        climate because it's surrounded by mountains
        on all sides. The valley rarely gets snow and
        most snow is gone the same day. Summers are
        normally hot and dry.

- Lewiston is a manufacturing town, featuring several national manufacturers, including Vista Outdoors, Schweitzer Engineering Laboratories, and Clearwater Paper.

HELPFUL RESOURCES

https://www.nezpercecountymuseum.com/

https://visitlcvalley.com/

https://hellscanyon.net/

https://www.twistedvinewt.com/home/

PACKING AND PLANNING TIPS

A Week before Leaving

- Arrange for someone to take care of pets and water plants.

- Email and Print important Documents.

- Get Visa and vaccines if needed.

- Check for travel warnings.

- Stop mail and newspaper.

- Notify Credit Card companies where you are going.

- Passports and photo identification is up to date.

- Pay bills.

- Copy important items and download travel Apps.

- Start collecting small bills for tips.

- Have post office hold mail while you are away.

- Check weather for the week.

- Car inspected, oil is changed, and tires have the correct pressure.

- Check airline luggage restrictions.

- Download Apps needed for your trip.

Right Before Leaving

- Contact bank and credit cards to tell them your location.

- Clean out refrigerator.

- Empty garbage cans.

- Lock windows.

- Make sure you have the proper identification with you.

- Bring cash for tips.

- Remember travel documents.

- Lock door behind you.

- Remember wallet.

- Unplug items in house and pack chargers.

- Change your thermostat settings.

- Charge electronics and prepare camera memory cards.

READ OTHER
GREATER THAN A TOURIST
BOOKS

> TOURIST

Follow us on Instagram for beautiful travel images:
http://Instagram.com/GreaterThanATourist

Follow *Greater Than a Tourist* on Amazon.

CZYKPublishing.com

> TOURIST

At *Greater Than a Tourist*, we love to share travel tips with you. How did we do? What guidance do you have for how we can give you better advice for your next trip? Please send your feedback to GreaterThanaTourist@gmail.com as we continue to improve the series. We appreciate your constructive feedback. Thank you.

METRIC CONVERSIONS

TEMPERATURE

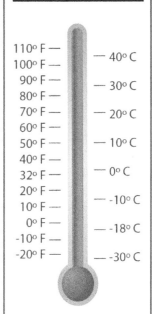

110° F —   — 40° C
100° F —
90° F —   — 30° C
80° F —
70° F —   — 20° C
60° F —
50° F —   — 10° C
40° F —
32° F —   — 0° C
20° F —
10° F —   — -10° C
0° F —
-10° F —   — -18° C
-20° F —   — -30° C

To convert F to C:

Subtract 32, and then multiply by 5/9 or .5555.

To Convert C to F:

Multiply by 1.8 and then add 32.

32F = 0C

LIQUID VOLUME

To Convert:.................Multiply by
U.S. Gallons to Liters................ 3.8
U.S. Liters to Gallons 26
Imperial Gallons to U.S. Gallons 1.2
Imperial Gallons to Liters....... 4.55
Liters to Imperial Gallons 22
1 Liter = .26 U.S. Gallon
1 U.S. Gallon = 3.8 Liters

DISTANCE

To convert ....Multiply by
Inches to Centimeters 2.54
Centimeters to Inches 39
Feet to Meters...................... .3
Meters to Feet 3.28
Yards to Meters 91
Meters to Yards 1.09
Miles to Kilometers 1.61
Kilometers to Miles............ .62
1 Mile = 1.6 km
1 km = .62 Miles

WEIGHT

1 Ounce = .28 Grams
1 Pound = .4555 Kilograms
1 Gram = .04 Ounce
1 Kilogram = 2.2 Pounds

TRAVEL QUESTIONS

- Do you bring presents home to family or friends after a vacation?

- Do you get motion sick?

- Do you have a favorite billboard?

- Do you know what to do if there is a flat tire?

- Do you like a sun-roof open?

- Do you like to eat in the car?

- Do you like to wear sun glasses in the car?

- Do you like toppings on your ice cream?

- Do you use public bathrooms?

- Did you bring a cell phone and does it have power?

- Do you have a form of identification with you?

- Have you ever been pulled over by a cop?

- Have you ever given money to a stranger on a road trip?

- Have you ever taken a road trip with animals?

- Have you ever gone on a vacation alone?

- Have you ever run out of gas?

- If you could move to any place in the world, where would it be?

- If you could travel anywhere in the world, where would you travel?

- If you could travel in any vehicle, which one would it be?

- If you had three things to wish for from a magic genie, what would they be?

- If you have a driver's license, how many times did it take you to pass the test?

- What are you the most afraid of on vacation?

- What do you want to get away from the most when you are on vacation?

- What foods smell bad to you?

- What item do you bring on every trip with you away from home?

- What makes you sleepy?

- What song would you love to hear on the radio when you're cruising on the highway?

- What travel job would you want the least?

- What will you miss most while you are away from home?

- What is something you always wanted to try?

- What is the best road side attraction that you ever saw?

- What is the farthest distance you ever biked?

- What is the farthest distance you ever walked?

- What is the weirdest thing you needed to buy while on vacation?

- What is your favorite candy?

- What is your favorite color car?

- What is your favorite family vacation?

- What is your favorite food?

- What is your favorite gas station drink or food?

- What is your favorite license plate design?

- What is your favorite restaurant?

- What is your favorite smell?

- What is your favorite song?

- What is your favorite sound that nature makes?

- What is your favorite thing to bring home from a vacation?

- What is your favorite vacation with friends?

- What is your favorite way to relax?

- Where is the farthest place you ever traveled in a car?

- Where is the farthest place you ever went North, South, East and West?

- Where is your favorite place in the world?

- Who is your favorite singer?

- Who taught you how to drive?

- Who will you miss the most while you are away?

- Who if the first person you will contact when you get to your destination?

- Who brought you on your first vacation?

- Who likes to travel the most in your life?

- Would you rather be hot or cold?

- Would you rather drive above, below, or at the speed limited?

- Would you rather drive on a highway or a back road?

- Would you rather go on a train or a boat?

- Would you rather go to the beach or the woods?

TRAVEL BUCKET LIST

1.

2.

3.

4.

5.

6.

7.

8.

9.

10.

NOTES

Made in United States
Orlando, FL
16 November 2023